Valerie Murray

LES MURRAY
Killing the Black Dog

Les Murray is the author of thirteen books of poetry. His collection *Subhuman Redneck Poems* received the T. S. Eliot Prize, and in 1998 Queen Elizabeth presented him with the Queen's Gold Medal for Poetry. He lives on a farm on the north coast of New South Wales, Australia.

Killing the Black Dog

A Memoir of Depression

Les Murray

Farrar, Straus and Giroux

New York

Farrar, Straus and Giroux
18 West 18th Street, New York 10011

Copyright © 2009 by Les Murray
All rights reserved
Distributed in Canada by D&M Publishers, Inc.
Printed in the United States of America
Originally published in 2009 by Black Inc., Australia
Published in the United States by Farrar, Straus and Giroux
First American edition, 2011

Library of Congress Cataloging-in-Publication Data
Murray, Les A., 1938–
    Killing the black dog : a memoir of depression / Les Murray.— 1st American ed.
        p.   cm.
    Includes indexes.
    ISBN 978-0-374-18106-2 (alk. paper)
    1. Depression, Mental—Poetry.   2. Murray, Les A., 1938–   I. Title.

PR9619.3.M83K55 2011
821'.914—dc22

                                                                2010033509

Designed by Thomas Deverall

www.fsgbooks.com

1   3   5   7   9   10   8   6   4   2

To the need of God

Contents

*

Killing the Black Dog

Killing the Black Dog

ON THE LAST DAY OF 1985, I went home to live in Bunyah, the farming valley I had left some twenty-nine years earlier. My wife and our younger children followed two days later. My father had acquired an old forty-acre selector's block some ten years previously, and we'd built a house for him and for family visits from Sydney. In 1981, we'd extended this in preparation for a move which then got delayed by a family emergency, the diagnosis of autism in our fourth child. But now at last I was going home, to care for my father in his old age and to live in the place from which I'd always felt displaced. What I didn't know was that I was heading home in order to go mad.

All went well for the first year and most of the second. My wife had agreed to move on a year's trial, but after a couple of months she said she loved the new life and would stay indefinitely. We found better school arrangements for Alexander than any we'd found in Sydney after he'd finished with the Autistic Association's marvellous special school in Forestville. Modern communications made it just as easy for me to carry on my writing career out of Bunyah as out of Sydney; a great change that had occurred in my absence was that, where once you had to be a housewife, farmer, farm worker or timber hand to live in the bush, now all sorts of trades and none were followed there without social pressure. At first I suffered no more than the normal background depressiveness of a writer, plus the irritable defensiveness that came from a bitter division in the literary world which had begun in the late 1960s, between the so-called Generation of '68 and those who served it throughout the Australian cultural world and a minority of us whom it demonised as its opponents. The tears which had appeared as an absolute in a mysterious figure who wept in Martin Place, in a poem called 'An Absolutely Ordinary Rainbow', which I'd written a few years after my first depressive breakdown at the end of the fifties, now seemed to have dried in my imagination. I enjoyed discovering that I was still attuned to the wry subtleties of conversation around my region, though I'd missed a whole generation of my friends' and cousins' kids. But if home conceals Old Bad Stuff you had not mastered the first time around, going back there, perhaps especially as you approach your fifties, is an invitation to crisis. Mine started with a well-attended poetry reading at the bowling club in Taree in early 1988.

In many ways, it was a triumph for a local celebrity. The member of parliament for our electorate was there, the dignitaries of all the service clubs were there – at the end of the evening, I was presented with the Paul Harris Fellowship of Rotary International, which I understand is a rare honour for a non-member of the organisation – and upwards of a hundred and fifty guests had come to hear me. Among them was a former schoolmate from the Leaving Certificate class of 1956 at Taree High School. This woman cheerfully recalled to me one of the nicknames she had bestowed on me thirty-odd years previously, and within a day or two I began to come apart. I started to suffer painful tingling in my fingers, I began to slip into bouts of weeping as I drove my car – 'What the hell is this?' I asked myself, but the cause of the tears wouldn't come into focus. In the middle of that year, my ongoing breakdown threw up a very happy symptom: cigars suddenly gave me up. From being an eight-cigar-a-day smoker, I suddenly became unable to endure the taste of tobacco; it was worse than burning rubber, and this change has been lasting. Around the same time, savage indigestion racked me throughout a fortnight's tour in Ireland, then ebbed away; I'd never previously suffered this complaint at all. I'd always led a crowding mental life, but now my mind became congested, jammed with ideas I couldn't formulate clearly or nimbly enough, so that they tumbled over each other and made me incoherent. During a week's residency at La Trobe University around September that year, I faced at a seminar a nasty post-graduate student who had published an insulting study of my work, mocking me for grief at my mother's death many years before, and I found I couldn't denounce him effectively, or defend myself. I did go on writing poetry during this whole period, however, and the last poem I wrote before the crisis which would get my illness diagnosed was the title poem of a book called *Dog Fox Field* (1990). Several poems in the latter part of that book reflect my mental state, being over-concentrated and under-explained in ways not caused by experiment.

Driving home from La Trobe, I had several readings to give, and I managed to give them without trouble. In Canberra, I scored a parking ticket, which my wife got me off on a plea of insanity. Because just after my fiftieth birthday, I went to her complaining of chest pains and she drove me to Casualty at Taree Base Hospital. From my slow steady pulse, she deduced that I wasn't having a heart attack at all, but you don't ignore chest pains, and anyway I was badly in need of reassurance. Casualty took one look at my corpulence and my greying bald head and put me onto the monitor and an intravenous drip; within half an hour I found myself among the truly sick on the hospital's fourth floor, in the cardiac ward. It has the best view in its small city, but few up there are looking. 'Gooday, Les,' said a voice I hadn't heard since my early teens at Nabiac Central School. 'Remember me? I'm Arthur Bussey.' 'I do remember you, Arthur. How are you, if that's not a silly question?' 'I'm all right now, but see that table over there? I died four times on that bastard the other night. The old shockers brought me back, though.' Right after that, the duty priest turned up and offered me the last rites of the Catholic Church. I wavered for a moment, not sure whether things were that serious; my chest pains had mysteriously vanished. 'If you're on this ward, you're serious enough!' the Father said brusquely, and fetched out his anointing oils.

Eventually on that scary night, I got to sleep. Next morning, one of the first people I met announced herself cheerfully as the Blood Sister. 'I know you: you're Alex's dad,' she exclaimed, tapping off a blood sample. 'My husband's his teacher.' Every conceivable test was carried out on me and my fluids, and nothing at all untoward turned up. Not even my cholesterol was out of whack, amazing in one who loves to eat the stuff thickly spread on bread. 'You haven't had a heart attack,' I was told at morning tea time, 'and you don't even seem likely to have one. But you've had something, and we suspect it was a panic attack.' 'What's that?' I asked, never having heard the term before. 'The psychiatrist is probably the best man to explain that to you,' I heard. 'I'm giving you a referral to him.' That same day, I fronted Dr Mike Richardson, inventor of the excellent rooming-in system of care for mental patients by which they spend their periods of acute illness in special rooms at local hospitals and are cared for by a spouse or relative who can act as their go-between with the hospital staff. It's a method adapted from the Third World and has spread from Taree to more than a dozen towns and cities Australia-wide. Dr Richardson began by giving me a short lecture on the brain chemistry of depressive illness, starting off arrestingly with the words, 'If you had an accident driving home and we sectioned your brain in the post-mortem, we'd find the chemistry in there quite different from that in a normal healthy brain.' He explained about overproduction of adrenalin in a sort of jammed, dysfunctional version of the fight-or-flight reflex common to all animals, and how after its adrenalin rush the brain broke the hormone down into the wrong sorts of neurotransmitters. Was this caused by one's troubles? I asked him, or did it cause those troubles? A chicken-and-egg question, I was told; both possibilities were real. Some people probably were born with the tendency to this kind of hormone malfunction, and life then supplied the subject matter for their neuroses; others probably stressed their system hard enough and long enough to bring on the bad chemistry. I suspect I belong to the former group. Even when I was a baby, my parents were shocked by the paroxysmal rages I could fall into; only a warm bath would calm me down. And many of the Murrays, men of my father's and grandfather's generations, were prone even as adults to howling, bellowing rages audible over half of our valley. Whether by convention or better self-control, women never seemed to perform in this way – in local usage, the word 'performing' was a disdainful term for excesses of public rage or grief. My furies seem to have subsided after infancy, returning just a few times in my adolescence – or so I would once have described it. Now I suspect that, like very many inherently depressive people, I simply lost the anger contest after babyhood, to bigger contestants, and learned to secrete my rage deep inside where it would do me maximum harm.

In the first months and years after my 1988 breakdown, I made little progress against the disease I had taken to calling the Black Dog. This was Winston Churchill's name for his depression, but the term has an ancestry reaching back past Mephistopheles' first disguise in Goethe's *Faust* Part I, to mediaeval lore of familiars and spirit possession. According to my psychiatrist, much of the most accurate scientific writing on depression and indeed on morbid psychology in general before our own age is to be found in mediaeval demonologies. I did learn a simple breathing technique, from Dr Claire Weekes's writings, which got rid of the tingling in my fingers by reducing the acidity of my blood. This acidity results from over-breathing, sucking in an excess of air in preparation for a battle or a panic flight that never happens. Every day, though, sometimes more than once a day, sometimes all day, a coppery taste in my mouth, which I termed intense insipidity, heralded a session of helpless, bottomless misery in which I would lie curled in a foetal position on the sofa with tears leaking from my eyes, my brain boiling with a confusion of stuff not worth calling thought or imagery: it was more like shredded mental kelp marinaded in pure pain. During and after such attacks, I would be prostrate with inertia, as if all my energy had gone into a black hole. This extreme boneless inanition I'd experienced before, during what is called a 'benign' breakdown, which started around the end of 1959 and ended quite suddenly in mid-1962. There is a case of it in Günter Grass's novel *The Tin Drum*, when the anti-hero Oscar Matzerath after the Second World War has a period of monarchism, in which he worships an image of Queen Elizabeth II and lives on pasta which he cooks over a gas ring within reach of his bed. I had days when I spent a whole morning or afternoon raising the energy to walk to the next room for a book.

In my first period of breakdown, it was still the Amphetamine Age, a carryover from the Second World War, which had been fought and won not entirely but pretty substantially on Benzedrine. The Sydney University doctor thought Dexedrine and methedrine were good for us, and prescribed them like sweets to help us through exams; I used them to regain my verve and get from golf links to building sites – my down-and-out sleeping coverts – and to power my Bohemian days around the university and downtown. Now the bitter white or purple heart-racers were a distant memory, and the only drug that ever helped me was a cousin of Valium called Xanax. This was capable of taking the worst intensity out of a panic attack, or of reducing my phobia about roads with a drop on one side to the point where I could drive along the milder ones. I tried not to depend on it though, and several times phoned Dr Richardson from the very pit of terror to have my hypochondria soothed. A habit that persisted for years was my surreptitious taking of my pulse, often dozens of times a day, but three or four phantom heart attacks in a day was not un-common, and every few weeks or months I'd have a big full-dress one. Only once, however, in those bad early years did I actually persuade people to rush me to Casualty. That was one night when I happened to be staying over at our old place in Chatswood, where my eldest daughter then still lived. She and a Chinese-Australian former nurse who shared the house drove me to Royal North Shore Hospital, where the kindly registrar on duty talked me down and gently refused me an ECG exam-ination. And of course he was right. Varying this diet of dra-matic inner turmoil was what I came to call the 4 a.m. Show, the pre-dawn darkness in which you wake and lie sleepless till dawn, your troubles and terrors ripping into you with a gusto allowed them by fatigue and the disappearance of proportion. Taking a Xanax at that hour will get you merciful oblivion, but as time goes on it will begin to drag you down into red-eyed grogginess after each bit of relief that it brings. Probably the best account of a 4 a.m. Show is Philip Larkin's uncompro-mising poem 'Aubade', which mercilessly presents an atheist's terror of death.

Apart from Xanax, no other drugs worked for me at all. Not Tofranil, not lithium, not Prozac, none of them. What did help were work, family, routine and talks with other sufferers. If God helped, and I imagine He did, He didn't tell me about it – or perhaps I simply couldn't hear Him if He did. It may be wiser not to hear the Divine when you are crazy: you may do extreme things and get it a bad name. I did attend Mass steadily throughout, under my wife's good influence. If I seem reluctant to attribute much help to God, it's because despair is of the very grain of depression. You feel *beneath* help, beneath the reach even of Godhead. A lot of seemingly irreligious people feel this way, too low down for faith. I didn't take up illicit or even licit drugs for relief, but I did gain some sympathy for those who did. Not that I'd been specially judgmental about them before. Scorn the hype, the fashion, the sticky glamour, but not their victims. During even the worst of it, I only cancelled out of one of my overseas tours, a Bicentenary one to New York a couple of weeks after my first phantom heart attack. Otherwise, when the Dog savaged me overseas, I took my Xanax and somehow kept going. And at home I cut down on writing prose pieces because they were more liable than poetry to be infiltrated with the colours of confusion and obsession. Poetry does not only require discipline, it is a discipline, and resists imbalance and turgidity by evaporating when they clamour to get in. I wrote some good prose in those years, but I had to be on guard against sideslips into the black kelp, and when I was utterly depleted I concentrated my resources around my essential art form, poetry, because it was what I'd bet my life on.

Family helped in a thousand ways, many of them better not described except under large headings like Mothering or Setting Straight or Advising Against Rashness. Don't make a scene: the poor waitress isn't to blame. Of course the traffic police are just collecting taxes from the motorists they trap but you won't beat them. One family joke that defused obsessions was the one about the *csúzli* (pronounced CHOOZ-li) which is Hungarian for a shanghai or slingshot. A ging, if you're from Western Australia. It concerns the poor obsessive who languishes in the madhouse because his whole life and energy are devoted to purloining rubber or elastic and making these devices. The board of assessors examines his mental state several times and sadly concludes he isn't ready for liberty, but one day he really looks much improved, neat, coherent in his speech, promising the earth if they will but let him go home. 'What will you do first of all if we release you?' 'Ah, I'll find myself a nice girl and invite her to dinner and the cinema.' 'And what then?' 'Then I'll look deep into her eyes and tell her my heart is longing for her.' I should tell you this is a very old story, from 1930s Budapest. The board excitedly asks, 'And then?' 'Then I'll take her home and we'll hug and kiss.' 'Yes, yes?' 'And then I'll start undressing her gently and lovingly. And I'll come to her panties, and I'll take them off, and I'll pull the elastic from them, and AAARRRH I'll make a shanghai . . .' In our family, any hobbyhorse, especially an unbalanced one, is a *csúzli*. As I often had to be reminded.

Only once did I fall so ill within reach of home that I had to phone and beg to be rescued. I'd taken the older car we had to Taree for garage work, but the Dog leapt upon me and I couldn't endure to stay in town, so Valerie drove her car in to get me. On the way home, she asked me to wear my seat belt, but I regard those as forced medication even on my sunny days, and the very existence of any aspect of the Nanny State or its goon police that day incensed me almost to the point of lifting my head off my chest. And sure enough, ten kilometres out of town, a busy highway-patrol cop buzzed alongside us on a motorbike.

'I observe, sir,' he said in the usual knuckleduster tones of official politeness, 'that you are not wearing a seat belt.' 'I've got a medical exemption from wearing them,' I replied truthfully, for at that time I had. 'Can I see that document, sir?' 'It's in my other pants at home, I'm sorry. I can bring it in, or send a photocopy of it.' 'Ah, I have to see it visually, sir.' At this point I actually looked at him and said, 'Shoot me. My offence is clearly unpardonable, and I'm sick of my life. Blow me away with that cannon of yours!' Whereupon the young man leaped back on his bike and roared off without another word. I was just beginning to come out of the episode that had crippled me in town, and I said shakily to Valerie, who had anxiously added to the man that 'my husband is very ill,' 'I wonder if I could have done that sane?' I tried, a couple of years later, but the magic was gone and it didn't wash.

Mental illness is apt to make you into a bore. I had to beware of telling people about my condition, and especially I had to beware of talking about it in its own ghastly demeaning style. My major slip-up in this regard was a lecture I gave one day, unwisely in the very place where the Black Dog had lain buried: Taree High School. Two other speakers on themes of social handicap preceded me and did well, speaking in dignified terms of rejections overcome and satisfactions attained; one was the local artist Russel Saunders, founder of the Birripi Arts Collective, an Aboriginal group which has produced some very fine painting and animal sculpture. When I spoke, though, my pain got the better of me, flowing down the years from the mid-fifties into my voice and my posture, causing me to accuse and whine. The talk was to teachers from the whole region, and it ensured that I didn't get any more invitations to high schools on our part of the coast for years, though my cousin Gai Hoddinott, who teaches English at Forster High, said her colleagues had enjoyed the drama. It was an early, failed attempt at something I'd have to do internally before I could risk it again in public: a close questioning of past trauma to learn what damage it had done and what conclusions could be drawn from it. A talking cure rather than a chemical one, but not according to the pre-cut schema of Freud, and not talking to another, but to myself. The difficulty would be to get the murk and distorting charge out of the talk and clarify it through repetition till I could 'hear' it and think straight about it.

In the first few years, this was impossible, and after a few tentative tries at submitting the whole mass of pain to poetic examination, which produced some knotted unclear poems in the latter part of *Dog Fox Field*, I turned the instrument of poetry away from all that for the length of one whole book, written substantially in 1990 and 1991. The heart of this book, *Translations from the Natural World* (1992), was a sequence of forty poems titled 'Presence' and subtitled 'Translations from the Natural World', in which I gave my stupid self a rest and tried to enter imaginatively into the life of non-human creatures and somehow translate that life into human speech. The first and longest poem in the book, though, was a rhymed one titled 'Kimberley Brief', which recounted the course of a trip I made with Michael Leunig to far north-western Australia. Leunig's wry fantastical cartoons are internationally known; what is less well known but might easily be guessed is that he's a long-term depressive. I derived great benefit from talking with him, as we often do when the pain and its terms are shared and there can be no more nonsense about Getting a Grip on Yourself. We gave each other permission to be ill, a necessary precondition of being cured. I'm convinced that stoicism is never the answer to anything, being nothing more than a cruel, callous encouragement to people to devour each other, a powerful ally of sadists and tyrants keen to get people to endure things which should be firmly refused as unendurable. Courage, indeed! Desensitisation and bully-training, rather. Another sufferer was a neat, efficient, warm-hearted professional lady in Scotland whose four years in Hell with the

Black Dog no one could ever have guessed at – or heard about past her English reserve. It was she who convinced me of what the handbooks claimed, that the illness can and mostly does run its course and vanish. If it doesn't cause us to suicide before it stops. I was never inclined to suicide, and did not contemplate it, but I remembered good friends who had gone that way at Sydney University, and a friend who declared a strong belief in the life of the world to come and a belief that life in this world doesn't work. She was out to shed her anguish by shedding the mortal life which fuelled it, and looked to a fresh start in Heaven. I'll never blame her, and if you do, you've never been where she and I have been and you can't say anything meaningful to us or about us.

By the first half of 1992, the crowding frequency of panic attacks and helpless downers was beginning to ease and take on a rhythm. I was almost always laid low on a Saturday, but there were now days when I felt well and not even exhausted. I was becoming what is called cyclothymic, that is, my depressive phenomena were taking on a regular pattern. This made it possible for me to open a new phase of my fight against the disease. I would come at it afresh with the instruments of poetry, plus an intense effort of recollection: around the same time I also embarked on a long work of fiction in verse which I might never have essayed without the disease. This is a verse novel that will only get its name when it is finished, I hope in a year or so from now; it concerns a German-Australian sailor named Fred Boettcher, from Dungog, who sees some Armenian women being burned alive in 1915 in Turkey during the Armenian genocide which inspired Hitler. Fred and his shipmates are unable to stop the atrocity, and as a result he loses, for many years, his cutaneous sensation. He can't feel, in other words. His unconscious can, and protects him from harm. 'My inner man can feel, but he doesn't tell me what he's feeling,' as Fred explains the matter to Marlene Dietrich. The seed of the narrative was a poem by one Siamanto (pseudonym of the Armenian poet Atom Yarjanian, 1878–1915) who himself died in the genocide; in the poem, which is titled 'The Dance', a German witness is speaking about a group of twenty Armenian wives dragged from their houses by a mob to be insulted and savaged:

> *The twenty sank exhausted to the ground.*
> *'Get up!' The naked swords flickered like snakes.*
> *Then someone fetched a pitcher of kerosene.*
> *Human justice, I spit in your face.*
> *Without delay the twenty were anointed.*
> *'Dance!' roared the mob; 'This is sweeter*
> *than the perfumes of Arabia!'*
> *They touched the naked women with a torch.*
> *And there was dancing. The charred bodies rolled.*

I have always been fascinated by the question of how it is possible, even with the help of deadening stoicism or maniac laughter, to live with the darker aspects of human frightfulness. And that's Fred's problem too. His reaction makes him enormously strong, a veritable Teutonic superman at times, because he can't detect how much the effort costs – but I'm still writing the book, and won't pre-empt it.

Introspection showed me that I'd been a sub-clinical depressive for pretty well all of my life, with two bouts of acute illness, the one starting at the end of the fifties and evoked in the early poem 'Recourse to the Wilderness' and a recent poem titled 'The Head-Spider', and the other starting in 1988 and which I was still in. Several people had sent me copies of William Styron's remarkable memoir of his depressive breakdown, *Darkness Visible*. Like me he had suffered the loss of his mother in childhood, but I thought his diagnosis of depression as arising from uncompleted grieving rather simplistic, not likely to apply in all cases. His descriptions of being savaged by the Black Dog and turned into a great baby utterly dependent on his wife were spot-on, however. In my own case, the weight of grief had been heavy on my parents before it came to me. My mother had lost her father in 1930 when she was fifteen years old, and her family had, in that Depression year, crashed from affluence to want. My father did not get on well with his own father, a depressive who medicated his condition with a bottle of spirits a day and often went out with his friends and relations to get properly drunk. Dad resented the way his father, exploiting family feeling, had paid him no wages for eight years' savagely hard work as a timber-getter and bullock-driver. Now he'd been set up, without capital, on a small farm of his father's for which he had to pay rent, and my parents' venture into dairy farming collided with a wartime series of severe droughts and shortages. I was the only child they had; my birth was induced, and ever afterwards my mother had miscarriages, the last of which caused her death. She had begun haemorrhaging, and our too-antique car was out of service, and the Taree doctor in charge of ambulance services wouldn't send the ambulance. Dr Skinner apparently thought the bush folk were using the ambulance as a bit of a taxi service, but the real truth was that he didn't think us important enough to have it.

I should have mentioned a couple of long paragraphs ago the trick I devised from talks with Dr Richardson for riding out head-storms and phantom heart attacks: I learned as it were to lie down below them, too low and flat for them fully to reach me, and to tell them as they raged above me *You're an illusion. You're just crazed chemistry.* This was hard to do, but it was better than rolling helplessly in the blast of an inner hurricane, crashing into mental kerbstones and buildings, spinning down fictive mean streets with the whole torrent of dust and waste paper. As I became more capable of real introspection, the need for this trick diminished, and a new enemy I had to guard against was victim-addiction, the sick love of our symptoms that causes us to clutch them to us and indulge them. Amazing, you'd think, but adrenalin is addictive, as they could tell you at the Bathurst car races or a thousand other vortexes of excitement. (I know that should be 'vortices' but that form simply doesn't *look* like the plural of 'vortex'.) Addiction, as I say in a pivotal poem, is a cage we lust to climb repeatedly into, because it's dramatic and poignant and fills us with hideous importance in our own eyes. It feels like significance, and is better than emptiness. 'Corniche' is my answer, in a way, to Larkin's 'Aubade'; I'm not sure he knew, or fully knew, that he was describing a depressive attack. My reply to him is that of one who knows that the horror is driven by our illusion-hormone. Switching off that hormone and its effects may be one of the central tasks of religion.

In facing my personal inner history, I had to look at some dark stuff. I had to remember what had felt like a growing dislike of me on the part of my poor mother, as her miscarriages ate her happiness away, and to recall a nightmare sense on my part, which I may not have arrived at wholly on my own, that the disasters I was never told about were in fact my fault, for being born and for the circumstances of my delivery. I had to recall the frequent harsh floggings I got for being a bad boy, in an age when flogging children was still an ordinary, accepted thing, especially among working people. You might say it was as much part of proletarian culture as the balalaika, except that we'd never heard of balalaikas. My aunt did have a good show-horse named Timoshenko, for the Soviet marshal. Floggees commonly pass on their stripes, and my father had been a prime floggee, whipped in drunken rages by his father and in cold experimental sessions by his elder brother, till he learned to outrun him. I had to recall that for a few years I'd been given to whipping our first two children, who never really deserved it. I still recall my sudden revulsion at this, and the way I dropped the habit forever in the early seventies. It was too late, though, and the justifiable resentment our eldest feel has been severe. I had to remember how my wife and our eldest two children suffered flaking dermatitis on their knuckles for years because of the stress I caused them. I never had the dermatitis back then, but it appeared on my forehead and down both sides of my nose after 1988, when the scab-picking self-disfigurement I'd practised since early childhood also got worse. I had to remember my terrible outbursts of ire over trifles, and how I'd sometimes terrorised my family on long car trips. The worst way to have chronic depression is to have it unconsciously, to be in a burning rage and not know you are angry. Was I angry at my mother for, as we'd say in an Irish-derived Australian idiom, dying on me? Maybe, but that did feel a bit literary and Freudian, with no sense of truth under it. I discovered I had been furious at my father for sinking into broken-hearted grief when my mother died, a grief he nourished and refused to give up till the day of his own death some forty-four years later. I hated how I'd had to become my own parents and get through adolescence with little help, continuing to play childhood games with my cousin Ray well beyond the natural end of those, so as to shut out the helpless half-adulthood that had fallen on me along with the guilt of matricide and the strong family message that sex had now been *confirmed* as sinful by directly causing death. Never do it, my unconscious told my body: you'll kill the victim.

Apart from Dr Richardson, I suppose my only other psychiatrist was Hannibal Lecter, in *The Silence of the Lambs*. He impressed upon me that for self-examination to work, you must tell the exact truth, suppressing nothing. That's what I'm telling you here, but I do suppress bits that would violate others' privacy. I can do this because you aren't curing me, rather I'm telling you what did help me, and my own part in it. The Lecter character also mentioned that unhappy children liable to go to the bad often show it early by hurting animals and setting fires. I'd done both, but not much more than other boys around our way, where burning off dry grass and scrub was a practice and a sport going back to Aboriginal times, and torturing beasts was in part a by-product of the endless war on rabbits and other pests. In the poem 'A Torturer's Apprenticeship', however, I'd already voiced an old suspicion that but for the coming of Christ and poetry into my life at the end of my teens I might have become something rather awful, worse even than the epithets some critics assign to me.

Being an only child and mildly autistic, as I now realise I am – not for nothing am I the father of a moderately high-performing Asperger, as we now call autistic savants – I'd grown up with no social skills at all, beyond boasting and showing off and giving lectures about things I knew or pretended to know. All the same, though I only met children on a regular basis from the age of nine, when I started school, I didn't fare badly among the rather innocent kids of my own culture, in the country and village schools around our district. No one bullied me or called me by a nickname till, after a year's lay-off following the Intermediate Certificate, I resumed my education at Taree High at the age of sixteen. There, among neatly dressed town kids for the first time, I made all the wrong opening moves and promptly died for it. I came on as friendly, puppy-like, as well as a Brain and a show-off, and the unanimous verdict was that I must be reminded constantly that I was fat and ridiculous. In the next two years, only one fellow student, a boy, ever called me by my real first name. To the rest, I was known as Murray or, more usually, by a plethora of fat nicknames; my then only slight corpulence outweighed any other characteristic, and was the only thing about me that was allowed to be talked of. Every sentence addressed to me had to allude to it. Some of the boys occasionally flagged from the sheer effort of this, but no girl ever broke ranks. Those who didn't go in for name-calling and hysterical bouts of coming on to me and then running away in shrieks of laughter to join their cheering fellows maintained a stony reserve in which they never met my eye or prolonged an exchange. I reacted to all this by pretending, to them and myself, that nothing untoward was happening, trying to confuse them by turning the other cheek. As we say in handicapped-child circles, I was Extinguishing the Behaviour. Turning the other cheek is hard, though, as I didn't know then; it has to be done with love, not disguised fury. And I never did extinguish the behaviour. Indeed, a few times when it showed signs of abating, in individuals, I suspect I stirred it up afresh to trap them in the childishness it entailed; I didn't want to release them into the adulthood they wanted to assume. To this day, I don't understand some parts of the campaign. For example, the only girl in the school who ever initiated a conversation with me was a cousin called Elizabeth King. The day after this friendly yarn, though, I saw her in the playground being earnestly Spoken To by other girls, all casting glances in my direction – and these were the last looks she ever did cast in my direction. She had seemingly got her peer-group orders, and I ceased to exist. And she wasn't even in my accursed year, but several years lower.

During the time I was dredging all of this up from the smouldering ash-pit of memory, our gentle second daughter was undergoing a similar nightmare at St Clare's, Taree's Catholic high school, which has a bit of cachet because it charges a fee and so keeps Aboriginal students out. There's nothing remotely Catholic in the demeanour of the school; that has long since been swamped by the non-Catholic kids who attend there. The Manning Valley is by all accounts a dangerous place for children. One local teenager a week, Dr Richardson told me, makes an attempt on their life. We saved Clare only when we found out what kids never tell you, that she was in peer trouble, and she is only now making a good recovery at the age of twenty-two. On the basis of her experience and mine, I wrote, at intervals, a series of poems which did both of us good. They were: 'Where Humans Can't Leave and Mustn't Complain', 'Rock Music', 'Burning Want' – the poem which more than any other unlocked the tumblers of my illness – and 'The Head-Spider', mentioned above. I'd disapproved of using poetry as personal therapy, but the Black Dog taught me better. Get sick enough, and you'll use any remedy you've got.

The upshot of my matricidal guilt and the two years of daily sexual rejection was a buried fury at sex and a terror of women that denied me all dalliance till well into my twenties, then abated only for one person, whom I married, and returned to protect all other women from me. I liked women, and enjoyed their company, but any movement towards the erotic filled me with desperate misgivings, and I would bolt. In the very early '60s, when the pill was coming in, a woman postgraduate student at Sydney University asked me why I hated women so much. I was dumbfounded, having been brought up on my mother's doctrine of strict equality of the sexes, and burbled some witless non-answer. A fiver a week from home, and then no allowance at all, prevented anything I'd have understood as courtship, but my terror went deeper than that. I feared they would die, by my fault; when abortion came in, I feared to cause one, but above all I feared the awful ridicule which would certainly greet any approach on my part. And even if one were allowed to mate, unbearable ridicule would follow; we saw this fear come true when militant feminism captured literature and the media. The culture filled up with raucous contempt of men, and Bob Ellis dragged me along to plays in which all men were inadequate, in crassly physical ways which male mythology had always feared. I arrived at my reticence without a shred of Catholicism, joining that Church only when I was twenty-four and married, though I had been drawn to it as early as my eighteenth year by its intransigent defiance of all ordinary contemporary thinking. The Sacrament, which it refused to water down to a mere metaphor, drew me especially; without such vertically steep walls of claim, where could we rejects go for shelter? By the time I'd been through the mill of the nascent Teen Age, I was no longer reachable by even the kindest of girls. One, sister of the only schoolmate who ever called me by my Christian name, was a little older than me and out of school, and it took me much desperate deflection and sheer boring motormouth to make her go away. She would have solved my problem, out of pity or generosity or maybe even affection, but I was too unconsciously furious to allow it. I was also, and remain, quite incapable of interpreting female signals, or distinguishing between flirting and what primatologists unpleasantly term presenting. I never dared assume a sexual invitation could be real, if directed at me.

The prime site of my illness, then, was sexual. Common enough. As I unearthed my buried troubles, I saw how closely bound up they were with features of modern society that I loathed, such as demonstrations, in which I always heard the echo of the schoolyard, or radicalisms which seemed to enlarge the schoolyard into a whole ideal world. In the chants of early militant feminism, I heard the accents of Taree High. In a column I used to write for the short-lived *Independent Monthly*, I coined the term 'erocide', meaning the deliberate destruction of a person's sexual morale, and speculated that we victims of that process probably outnumber all other victim-groups combined, but will never rise up and demand redress. We are too deeply shamed, and too darkly aware that those rejected for reproduction or pleasure are scapegoats for the pain which sex entails even among the attractive. I came to see that the tone of much in the Totalitarian Age that may just now be drawing to a close exactly resembles clinical depression. It is the secret co-opted fuel of many Causes, and is not exposed for what it is because it is as common, and exploitable, on one side of politics as on the other. If, as shrinks tell us, a fifth of all people in this stressed age will suffer at least one depressive episode in their lives, there is clearly an enormous pool of potential recruits

26

among people who haven't identified the real roots of their trouble and so will reliably hate substitutes or near-enough versions. We've all observed the desperate bored fatigue which overcomes activists when any topic not on their agenda is raised, or the bristling that arises when playful spin is put on their obsessions. If you are energy-depleted, it's natural that you will have time only for a manageable list of issues, insisting that all talk be about those, and in deadly earnest. At the heart of all the proclaimed love of abstractions and absolutes there is the characteristic inability to love actual persons, or to forgive them. Because they are usually the wrong persons, and we can only forgive as it were outwards, starting with those who are at the real source of our pain. We have to identify these, and face our own actions in respect of them, giving ourselves and them the benefit of proportion. So far as we know, neither we nor they had lived before, or come into the world well prepared for what we'd encounter. We couldn't always get it right first time.

By the time I'd completed the manuscript of my collection *Subhuman Redneck Poems*, so called in honour of my social class, I'd faced everything I could dredge up out of my lifelong disability, even the few times my poor father in the madness of his grief actually blamed me for my mother's death. I'd got down from several attacks a day to one or two a week, but I wasn't cured. Not inwardly, and not in my public life either. I was at home Up Home, but in the literary world I felt like a pariah, admired abroad but detested at home. The inner circles of the Australia Council knew me as their Token Fascist, and colleagues who were thought to be close to me found their careers did not prosper; they faced obstruction, bad reviews, lack of funding. Even advanced Catholic circles saw me as an enemy, and a convert who got a chair at Monash University for turning on me started what became a leftist 'line' by claiming I'd peaked as a poet decades before and had since declined; this in the teeth of a worldwide acceptance based squarely on my later work. To cap his efforts, he then put the rumour around in Melbourne that I was a secret antisemite. This was in 1988, and I only learned of it a decade later.

I was dejected about the immutably anti-rural bias of Australian intellectual culture, its unoriginality, its ever-belated servitude to foreign ideas. I thought I was down to six or eight friends, but most of all I was in despair at the fact that I'd used my best Sunday punch on my illness, putting it under strict poetic analysis, and still hadn't defeated it. God, whoever He was apart from being all that was best and strangest in Jesus, seemed content to leave me in the muck till I died, and let no one pull me out of there. But as in composing a poem or a sequence, anguished thought had perhaps set up the conditions for a deep inner shift in my life; first the urgent spells, then at last the magic. Because, ironically for one who spoke of brooding as 'eating my liver', I was struck down on 12 July 1996 by a liver abscess which came within a hair of killing me. I was transported in an ambulance – we had risen that far –

docked of a fifth of my liver when I'd been brought far enough back from the brink to allow it, and awakened to find my state funeral in full swing. Cards, letters, flowers and phone calls had flowed in from everywhere, from home and around the world, and I'd been in the papers, with weekly reports on my condition – it was the biggest demonstration of public love and concern that will ever come my way, I'm sure, and only the Generation of '68 stayed aloof from it. Despite that, it was an affirmation I'd needed, and as I lay weakly on my hospital bed I started composing, in my head because my writing hand was still too shaky, a poem on the bombing of Manchester and the destruction of my British publisher's office in that city.

Even before I was conscious of the public affirmation, I discovered that the Black Dog had left me. And in the months since I came home, he hasn't returned. My thinking is no longer jammed and sooty with resentment. I no longer wear only stretch-knit clothes and drawstring pants. I no longer come down with bouts of weeping or reasonless exhaustion. And I no longer seek rejection in a belief that only bitterly conceded praise is reliable. I'd always seen women in the un-wounded parts of my mind as simply fellow humans: now I may be able to see them that way altogether. If I have a regret, in the sudden youth and health of my mind in its fifty-eighth year, it is that I've got well so late in my life, as in a poem I started writing for my wife Valerie before the Big Sick and finished after it:

A Reticence

After a silver summer
of downpours, cement-powder autumn
set in its bag. Lawns turned crunchy
but the time tap kept dribbling away.

The paddocks were void as that evening
in early childhood when the sun
was rising in the west,
round and brimming as the factory furnace door,

as I woke up after sickness.
Then it was explained to me
that I'd slept through from morning
and I sobbed because I'd missed that day,

my entire lovely day.
Without you, it might have been a prophecy.

1997

AFTERWORD

IT IS NOW ELEVEN YEARS since I wrote the lecture which became *Killing the Black Dog*. The book has enjoyed a steady sale since it appeared. This new edition, however, allows me to correct an error which has hung on its heels for a long time. When I came back from my coma in 1996, sheer euphoria of survival dismissed the depression fairly completely for a couple of years, and deceived me that it was gone. But I was wrong. As the last years of the twentieth century counted down, I came to realise that the atmosphere and themes of the disease had merely taken a holiday. Slowly but surely they crept back on me. They would never again be as savage as in my worst years – though at times they would send symptoms as bad as any I'd ever suffered. The returning illness would once again shoot crippling arrows into my life, keeping me from literary occasions, making me swear on TV, causing me to blaze up or wizen at any challenge. I was made to remember who still owned the game.

All was not dust and ashes: I had many more 'good' days than before my near-death. Occasional moments of equanimity surprised me. When I was set on by the entire Australian quality media in 1999 for writing a draft preamble to the Constitution for a prime minister they loathed, I was unperturbed. The text was intentionally aimed at their throat, proposing inter alia to ban rule by fashion and press hounding of dissenters, and they would be frantic to protect themselves. The editor of our one national daily later wrote to me to gloat that most of the letters he had printed against me had in fact been written in-house by his staff. More satisfying was the success I'd had a few years earlier with a poem I wrote ('A Deployment of Fashion') against the targeting of lone women by the media; the practice declined sharply straight away and has not really come back with its old brio. Best of all, I had been spared to finish *Fredy Neptune*. I'd fallen deadly sick in the middle of Book 4, and feared I'd never get to see how the story ended. Reception of the book was hostile in Australia, except among individuals, but major success gradually came from overseas.

In the short anthology which follows this, the last poem written before my liver collapse is 'One Kneeling, One Looking Down'. In the years since, I have gone on probing with my pen at matters raised by depression. Aphorism has helped me to clarify some things, including my relations with the political culture of my time and country. Which is by no means unanimously shared by my Australian readership; nearly all my quarrels have been with the official culture, of universities, media and government agencies, people who have agendas, or lines to toe. Since the turn of the millennium, it has grown harder even in Australia to keep the year 1968 afloat, and I have tried to grow away from even the memory of that horrible era. We Aspergers often show a tenacity in our battles which wiser minds would let go of. I sometimes think that our attitudes relate to our common inability to be spontaneous, or to experience love in any but narrow stereotyped ways. In the form of praise for instance, or its evil twin, opprobrium. Our difficulty in reading human signals is itself a Dog, closely related to the Black one.

After legal attempts to stop its publication, a biography of me by Peter Alexander appeared (*A Life in Progress*, 2000). Attacked as hagiography, it sold well, and revealed to me a few things I hadn't known. The major one was the reason for the terrible guilt which my wife realised had always accompanied my poor father's crippling grief. Out of an antique reticence concerning women's matters, plus an ingrained fear of gossip, he had been quite incapable of telling the town doctor, over an open phone line run by the most censorious busybody in our valley, that my mother was bleeding uncontrollably because of a miscarriage. 'She's havin a bad turn!' was all he could manage, and the doltish physician couldn't hear the desperation in his plea for the ambulance. Dad was caught in a trap of inner linguistic laws which he couldn't breach, and the doctor was deaf to the usage of people outside his class. 'Aboriginal people die that way all the time,' as an Aboriginal cousin from my mother's family told me when I told the story to her. This revelation, about the other half of my father's pain, helped me to forgive the awful negativity he had always shown to any opinion or initiative of mine. If I had not known his shame,

I hadn't known anything. His own main initiative in his remaining years of full strength was to give up farming in favour of brutally exhausting timber work, so as to deaden his emotions. Late in his life, when we moved home to live with him, the company of my wife and his grandchildren did much to lighten his mood before he died.

Peter Alexander also laid stress on the story, told to him by the former nurse who finally got the ambulance that frightful day, that my mother could have rallied and survived, in the week she spent in hospital before dying. My father had never told me this, and perhaps had never heard it himself. Peter suspected that despair had taken away my mother's will to live, so that she let her death happen. I was supposed to have taken this to mean that I was not worth surviving for. I was thus relieved, a few years after the biography came out, to get a letter from a doctor in Queensland, who did not give her surname, assuring me that a patient who has haemorrhaged massively *cannot* rally, because their body can't make new blood fast enough. We hadn't been abandoned. Alas, this letter came several years after Dad's death, but it helped me. Before we leave medical matters, a vagrant notion that has occurred to me a few times over the years since cigars gave me up forever is that tobacco may, historically, have played a large role in forestalling depressive breakdowns. I wouldn't recommend it, in the teeth of its now deadly ill repute, but smoking does stimulate blood circulation in the brain and maybe washes away bad neurotransmitters before they can have their full effects. It's like the way tobacco used to be prescribed for asthmatics: it did dilate their bronchioles and help them to breathe, even as it slowly wrecked their lungs.

If shedding the protection of tobacco to go acute helped speed up my depression towards a possible future recovery, being called on to talk in public about school bullying and the Black Dog over the years has helped me to insights and even flashes of gratitude. Most teachers know, for instance, that trying to support a bullied student is apt to get them a much worse time. Real help needs to be more sidelong. The English master and his wife at Taree High who introduced me to twentieth-century verse, way beyond the then curriculum, and the sports master who showed me modern Australian poetry, gave me the entrée to an art form they may have guessed might save me, even as my unconscious aptitude for it might have caused my miseries. Keith and the late Edith McLaughlin, and Les Lawrie, all three showed me how laterally true caregivers often have to think.

This long after the Big Sick, I'm no longer the glowering red-faced bully the artist Helen Potter painted in the early 1980s. This work, which shocked me then and still does so now, is in Taree's district art gallery. I hope I've kept the small lump of gold she allowed to exist in my head. My family reckon I became a much nicer person when I went acute, and I'm conscious now of being less obsessive much of the time, more capable of lateral thought even outside of poems, more at ease in my self-control. After an apparent remission, my fear of heights came back on me fiercely around 2004, and I had to do the shameful thing in 2005 and cancel out of a reading tour in Britain because I couldn't face the flight. A series of racking panics began to close in on me, too, such that for the first time in eighteen years I went back to the cardiologist just to be sure my heart hadn't started failing in what had become my late sixties. It hadn't, and it occurred to me to ask whether Lovan (fluoxetine), which our autistic son Alex had used in his early twenties to control outbursts of rage, would be safe for me to try. No other antidepressant drug had ever helped me, but I was assured Lovan was safe – and within weeks my acrophobia and nearly all of my regular low-grade gloom were gone. Acrophobia makes return visits when I'm unsure of the welcome awaiting me, but outside my own country I'm fine, and can once more earn half of our living from overseas readings, which are not haunted by home-grown ghosts.

I know now that you can't kill the Dog, and that thus my earlier account has the wrong title: it should be called *Learning the Black Dog*. Even before Lovan, I'd gained increments of self-esteem, and learned that treachery doesn't lurk behind every smile. I've become less afraid of Australian women, and less self-absorbed. At seventy, I'm at last more at ease with what Homer Simpson called his womanly needs. I've become freer from the aura of my parents' tragedy, and see it now more as a terrible ancient story, shining like floodwater through the hills of the 1940s, rather than pushing like freezing silt water into my mouth and nose. I've had a rehearsal of death and still know that I can accomplish the real thing when it comes, though dying didn't cure me the first time as I briefly thought it had. What I still do mourn is the terrible waste of energy the Dog has exacted from me, over my lifetime and especially in my twenty horror years, and how much more I might have achieved if I'd owned a single, healthy mind working on my side.

2009

The Black Dog Poems

An Absolutely Ordinary Rainbow

The word goes round Repins,
the murmur goes round Lorenzinis,
at Tattersalls, men look up from sheets of numbers,
the Stock Exchange scribblers forget the chalk in their hands
and men with bread in their pockets leave the Greek Club:
There's a fellow crying in Martin Place. They can't stop him.

The traffic in George Street is banked up for half a mile
and drained of motion. The crowds are edgy with talk
and more crowds come hurrying. Many run in the back streets
which minutes ago were busy main streets, pointing:
There's a fellow weeping down there. No one can stop him.

The man we surround, the man no one approaches
simply weeps, and does not cover it, weeps
not like a child, not like the wind, like a man
and does not declaim it, nor beat his breast, nor even
sob very loudly – yet the dignity of his weeping

holds us back from his space, the hollow he makes about him
in the midday light, in his pentagram of sorrow,
and uniforms back in the crowd who tried to seize him
stare out at him, and feel, with amazement, their minds
longing for tears as children for a rainbow.

Some will say, in the years to come, a halo
or force stood around him. There is no such thing.
Some will say they were shocked and would have stopped him
but they will not have been there. The fiercest manhood,
the toughest reserve, the slickest wit amongst us

trembles with silence, and burns with unexpected
judgements of peace. Some in the concourse scream
who thought themselves happy. Only the smallest children
and such as look out of Paradise come near him
and sit at his feet, with dogs and dusty pigeons.

Ridiculous, says a man near me, and stops
his mouth with his hands, as if it uttered vomit –
and I see a woman, shining, stretch her hand
and shake as she receives the gift of weeping;
as many as follow her also receive it

and many weep for sheer acceptance, and more
refuse to weep for fear of all acceptance,
but the weeping man, like the earth, requires nothing,
the man who weeps ignores us, and cries out
of his writhen face and ordinary body

not words, but grief, not messages, but sorrow,
hard as the earth, sheer, present as the sea –
and when he stops, he simply walks between us
mopping his face with the dignity of one
man who has wept, and now has finished weeping.

Evading believers, he hurries off down Pitt Street.

Midsummer Ice

Remember how I used
to carry ice in from the road
for the ice chest, half running,
the white rectangle clamped in bare hands
the only utter cold
in all those summer paddocks?

How, swaying, I'd hurry it inside
en bloc and watering, with the butter
and the wrapped bread precarious on top of it?
'Poor Leslie,' you would say,
'your hands are cold as charity – '
You made me take the barrow
but uphill it was heavy.

We'd no tongs, and a bag
would have soaked and bumped, off balance.
I loved to eat the ice,
chip it out with the butcher knife's grey steel.
It stopped good things rotting
and it had a strange comb at its heart,
a splintered horizon rife with zero pearls.

But you don't remember.

A doorstep of numbed creek water the colour of tears

but you don't remember.

I will have to die before you remember.

A Torturer's Apprenticeship

Those years trapped in a middling cream town
where full-grown children hold clear views
and can tell from his neck he's really barefoot
though each day he endures shoes,

he's what their parents escaped, the legend
of dogchained babies on Starve Gut Creek;
be friends with him and you will never
be shaved or uplifted, cool or chic.

He blusters shyly – poverty can't afford instincts.
Nothing protects him, and no one.
He must be suppressed, for modernity,
for youth, for speed, for sexual fun.

Also, believing as tacitly as he
that only dim Godly joys are equal
while the competitive, the exclusive
class pleasures are imperative evil

they see him as a nascent devil,
wings festering to life in his weekly shirt,
and daily go for the fist-and-finger
hung at the arch of keenest hurt.

Slim revenge of sorority. He must shoot birds,
discard the love myth and search for clues.
But for the blood-starred barefoot spoor
he found, this one might have made dark news.

An Era

The poor were fat and the rich were lean.
Nearly all could preach, very few could sing.
The fashionable were all one age, and to them
a church picnic was the very worst thing.

The Past Ever Present

Love is always an awarded thing
but some are no winners, of no awarding class.
Each is a song that they themselves can't sing.

For months of sundays, singlehanded under iron, with the flies,
they used to be safe from that dizzying small-town sex
whose ridicule brought a shamed evasion to their eyes.

Disdaining the relegated as themselves, they eyed the vividest
for whom inept gentleness without prestige was slow.
Pity even the best, then, when they're made second best.

Consider the self-sentenced who heel the earth round with
    shy feet
and the wallflower who weeps not from her eyes but her palms
and those who don't master the patter, or whom the codes
    defeat.

If love is always an awarded thing
some have cursed the judging and screamed off down old
    roads
and all that they killed were the song they couldn't sing.

Where Humans Can't Leave and Mustn't Complain

☞ for Becki and Clare

Where humans can't leave and mustn't complain
there some will emerge who enjoy giving pain.

Snide universal testing leads them to each one
who will shrivel reliably, whom the rest will then shun.

Some who might have been chosen, and natural police,
do routine hurt, the catcalling, the giving no peace,

but dull brilliance evolves the betrayals and names
that sear dignity and life like interior flames.

Hormones get enlisted, and consistency rehearsed
by self-avengers and failures getting in first,

but this is the eye of fashion. Its sniggering stare
breeds silenced accomplices. Courage proves rare.

This models revolution, this draws flies to stark pools.
This is the true curriculum of schools.

Rock Music

Sex is a Nazi. The students all knew
this at your school. To it, everyone's subhuman
for parts of their lives. Some are all their lives.
You'll be one of those if these things worry you.

The beautiful Nazis, why are they so cruel?
Why, to castrate the aberrant, the original, the wounded
who might change our species and make obsolete
the true race. Which is those who never leave school.

For the truth, we are silent. For the flattering dream,
in massed farting reassurance, we spasm and scream,
but what is a Nazi but sex pitched for crowds?

It's the Calvin SS: you are what you've got
and you'll wrinkle and fawn and work after you're shot
though tears pour in secret from the hot indoor clouds.

Corniche

I work all day and hardly drink at all.
I can reach down and feel if I'm depressed.
I adore the Creator because I made myself
and a few times a week a wire jags in my chest.

The first time, I'd been coming apart all year,
weeping, incoherent; cigars had given me up;
any road round a cliff edge I'd whimper along in low gear
then: cardiac horror. Masking my pulse's calm lub-dup.

It was the victim-sickness. Adrenalin howling in my head,
the black dog was my brain. Come to drown me in my breath
was energy's black hole, depression, compère of the predawn
    show
when, returned from a pee, you stew and welter in your
    death.

The rogue space rock is on course to snuff your world,
sure. But go acute, and its oncoming fills your day.
The brave die but once? I could go a hundred times a week,
clinging to my pulse with the world's edge inches away.

Laugh, who never shrank around wizened genitals there
or killed themselves to stop dying. The blow that never falls
batters you stupid. Only gradually do
you notice a slight scorn in you for what appals.

A self inside self, cool as conscience, one to be erased
in your final night, or faxed, still knows beneath
all the mute grand opera and uncaused effect –
that death which can be imagined is not true death.

The crunch is illusion. There's still no outside world
but you start to see. You're like one enthralled by bad art –
yet for a real onset, what cover! You gibber to Casualty,
are checked, scorned, calmed. There's nothing wrong with
     your heart.

The terror of death is not afraid of death.
Fear, pure, is intransitive. A Hindenburg of vast rage
rots, though, above your life. See it, and you feel flogged
but like an addict you sniffle aboard, to your cage,

because you will cling to this beast as it gnaws you,
for the crystal in its kidneys, the elixir in its wings,
till your darlings are the police of an immense fatigue.
I came to the world unrehearsed but I've learned some things.

When you curl, stuffed, in the pot at rainbow's end
it is life roaring and racing and nothing you can do.
Were you really God you could have lived all the lives
that now decay into misery and cripple you.

A for adrenalin, the original A-bomb, fuel
and punishment of aspiration, the Enlightenment's air-burst.
Back when God made me, I had no script. It was better.
For all the death, we also die unrehearsed.

The Beneficiaries

Higamus hogamus
Western intellectuals
never praise Auschwitz.
Most ungenerous. Most odd,
when they claim it's what finally
won them their centuries-
long war against God.

On Home Beaches

Back, in my fifties, fatter than I was then,
I step on the sand, belch down slight horror to walk
a wincing pit edge, waiting for the pistol shot
laughter. Long greening waves cash themselves, foam change
sliding into Ocean's pocket. She turns: ridicule looks down,
strappy, with faces averted, or is glare and families.
The great hawk of the beach is outstretched, point to point,
quivering and hunting. Cars are the surf at its back.
You peer, at this age, but it's still there, ridicule,
the pistol that kills women, that gets them killed, crippling
      men
on the towel-spattered sand. Equality is dressed, neatly,
with mouth still shut. Bared body is not equal ever.
Some are smiled to each other. Many surf, swim, play ball:
like that red boy, holding his wet T-shirt off his breasts.

Performance

I starred last night, I shone:
I was footwork and firework in one,

a rocket that wriggled up and shot
darkness with a parasol of brilliants
and a peewee descant on a flung bit;
I was busters of glitter-bombs expanding
to mantle and aurora from a crown,
I was fouettés, falls of blazing paint,
para-flares spot-welding cloudy heaven,
loose gold off fierce toeholds of white,
a finale red-tongued as a haka leap:
that too was a butt of all right!

As usual after any triumph, I was
of course inconsolable.

Memories of the Height-to-Weight Ratio

I was a translator in the Institute back
when being accredited as a poet
meant signing things against Vietnam.
For scorn of the bargain I wouldn't do it.

And the Institute was after me
to lose seven teeth and five stone in weight
and pass their medical. Three years I dodged
then offered the teeth under sacking threat.

From five to nine, in warm Lane Cove,
and five to nine again at night,
an irascible Carpatho-Ruthenian strove
with ethnic teeth. He claimed the bite

of a human determined their intelligence.
More gnash-power sent the brain more blood.
In Hungarian, Yiddish or Serbo-Croat
he lectured emotional fur-trimmers good,

clacking a jointed skull in his hand
and sent them to work face-numbed and bright.
This was my wife's family dentist. He
looked into my mouth, blenched at the sight,

eclipsed me with his theory of occlusion
and wrested and tugged. Pausing to blow
out cigarette smoke, he'd bite his only
accent-free mother tongue and return below

to raise my black fleet of sugar-barques
so anchored that they gave him tennis elbow.
Seven teeth I gave that our babies might eat
when students were chanting Make Love! Hey Ho!

But there was a line called Height-to-Weight
and a parallel line on Vietnam. When a tutor
in politics failed all who crossed that, and wasn't
dismissed, scholarship was back to holy writ.

Fourteen pounds were a stone, and of great yore so,
but the doctor I saw next had no schoolyard in him:
You're a natural weight-lifter! Come join my gym!
Sonnets of flesh could still model my torso.

Modernism's not modern: it's police and despair.
I wear it as fat, and it gnawed off my hair
as my typewriter clicked over gulfs and birch spaces
where the passive voice muffled enormity and faces.

But when the Institute started afresh
to circle my job, we decamped to Europe
and spent our last sixpence on a pig's head.
Any job is a comedown, where I was bred.

A Stage in Gentrification

Most Culture has been an East German plastic bag
pulled over our heads, stifling and wet,
we see a hotly distorted world
through crackling folds and try not to gag.

Sex, media careers, the Australian republic
and recruited depression are in that bag
with scorn of God, with self-abasement studies
and funding's addictive smelling-rag.

Eighty million were murdered by police
in the selfsame terms and spirit which nag
and bully and set the atmosphere
inside the East German plastic bag.

It wants to become our country's flag
and rule by demo and kangaroo court
but it's wearing thin. It'll spill, and twist
and fly off still rustling Fascist! Fascist!

and catch on the same fence as Hitler, and sag.

Burning Want

From just on puberty, I lived in funeral:
mother dead of miscarriage, father trying to be dead,
we'd boil sweat-brown cloth; cows repossessed the garden.
Lovemaking brought death, was the unuttered principle.

I met a tall adopted girl some kids thought aloof,
but she was intelligent. Her poise of white-blonde hair
proved her no kin to the squat tanned couple who loved her.
Only now do I realise she was my first love.

But all my names were fat-names, at my new town school.
Between classes, kids did erocide: destruction of sexual
    morale.
Mass refusal of unasked love; that works. Boys cheered as
    seventeen-
year-old girls came on to me, then ran back whinnying
    ridicule.

The slender girl came up on holidays from the city
to my cousins' farm. She was friendly and sane.
Whispers giggled round us. A letter was written as from me
and she was there, in mid-term, instantly.

But I called people 'the humans' not knowing it was rage.
I learned things sidelong, taking my rifle for walks,
recited every scene of *From Here to Eternity*, burned paddocks
and soldiered back each Monday to that dawning Teen age.

She I admired, and almost relaxed from placating,
was gnawed by knowing what she came from, not who.
Showing off was my one social skill, oddly never with her
but I dissembled feelings, till mine were unknown to me too

and I couldn't add my want to her shortfall of wantedness.
I had forty more years, with one dear remission,
of a white paralysis: she's attracted it's not real nothing is
    enough
she's mistaken she'll die go now! she'll tell any minute she'll
    laugh –

Whether other hands reached out to Marion, or didn't,
at nineteen in her training ward she had a fatal accident
alone, at night, they said, with a lethal injection
and was spared from seeing what my school did to the world.

Demo

No. Not from me. Never.
Not a step in your march,
not a vowel in your unison,
bray that shifts to bay.

Banners sailing a street river,
power in advance of a vote,
go choke on these quatrain tablets.
I grant you no claim ever,

not if you pushed the Christ Child
as President of Rock Candy Mountain
or yowled for the found Elixir
would your caste expectations snare me.

Superhuman with accusation,
you would conscript me to a world
of people spat on, people hiding
ahead of oncoming poetry.

Whatever class is your screen
I'm from several lower.
To your rigged fashions, I'm pariah.
Nothing a mob does is clean,

not at first, not when slowed to a media,
not when police. The first demos I saw,
before placards, were against me,
alone, for two years, with chants,

every day, with half-conciliatory
needling in between, and aloof
moral cowardice holding skirts away.
I learned your world order then.

The Head-Spider

Where I lived once, a roller coaster's range
of timber hills peaked just by our backyard cliff
and cars undulated scream-driven round its seismograph
and climbed up to us with an indrawn gasp of girls.

Smiles and yelling could be exchanged as they crested
then they'd pitch over, straining back in a shriek
that volleyed as the cars were snatched from sight
in the abyss, and were soon back. Weekdays they rested,

and I rested all days. There was a spider in my head
I'd long stay unaware of. If you're raped you mostly know
but I'd been cursed, and refused to notice or believe it.
Aloof in a Push squat, I thought I was moral, or dead.

Misrule was strict there, and the Pill of the day only ever
went into one mouth, not mine, and foamed a Santa-beard.
I was resented for chastity, and slept on an overcoat.
Once Carol from upstairs came to me in bra and kindness

and the spider secreted by girls' derision-rites to spare
women from me had to numb me to a crazed politeness.
Squeals rode the edge of the thrill building. Cartoonist
    Mercier
drew springs under Sydney. Push lovers were untrue on
    principle.

It's all architecture over there now. A new roller coaster
flies its ups and downs in wealth's face like an affront.
I've written a new body that only needs a reader's touch.
If love is cursed in us, then when God exists, we don't.

One Kneeling, One Looking Down

Half-buried timbers chained corduroy
lead out into the sand
which bare feet wincing Crutch and Crotch
spurn for the summer surf's embroidery
and insects stay up on the land.

A storm engrossing half the sky
in broccoli and seething drab
and standing on one foot over the country
burrs like a lit torch. Lightning
turns air to elixir at every grab

but the ocean sky is untroubled blue
everywhere. Its storm rolls below:
sand clouds raining on sacred country
drowned a hundred lifetimes under sea.
In the ruins of a hill, channels flow,

and people, like a scant palisade
driven in the surf, jump or sway
or drag its white netting to the tide line
where a big man lies with his limbs splayed,
fingers and toes and a forehead-shine

as if he'd fallen off the flag.
Only two women seem aware of him.
One says *But this frees us. I'd be a fool* –
Say it with me, says the other. *For him to revive*
we must both say it. Say Be alive. –

But it was our own friends who got
him with a brave shot, a clever shot. –
Those are our equals: we scorn them
for being no more than ourselves.
Say it with me. Say Be alive. –

Elder sister, it is impossible. –
Life was once impossible. And flight. And speech.
It was impossible to visit the moon.
The impossible's our summoning dimension.
Say it with me. Say Be alive again. –

The younger wavers. She won't leave
nor stop being furious. The sea's vast
catchment of light sends ashore a roughcast
that melts off every swimmer who can stand.
Glaring through slits, the storm moves inland.

The younger sister, wavering, shouts *Stay dead!*
She knows how impossibility
is the only door that opens.
She pities his fall, leg under one knee
but her power is his death, and can't be dignified.

Travels with John Hunter

We who travel between worlds
lose our muscle and bone.
I was wheeling a barrow of earth
when agony bayoneted me.

I could not sit, or lie down,
or stand, in Casualty.
Stomach-calming clay caked my lips,
I turned yellow as the moon

and slid inside a CAT-scan wheel
in a hospital where I met no one
so much was my liver now my dire
preoccupation. I was sped down a road

of treetops and fishing-rod lightpoles
toward the three persons of God
and the three persons of John Hunter
Hospital. Who said We might lose this one.

Twenty days or to the heat-death
of the Universe have the same duration:
vaguely half an hour. I awoke
giggling over a joke

about Paul Kruger in Johannesburg
and missed the white court stockings
I half remembered from my prone
still voyage beyond flesh and bone.

I asked my friend who got new lungs
How long were you crazy, coming back?
Five days, he said. Violent and mad.
Fictive Afrikaner police were at him,

not unworldly Oom Paul Kruger.
Valerie, who had sat the twenty days
beside me, now gently told me tales
of my time-warp. The operative canyon

stretched, stapled, with dry roseate walls
down my belly. Seaweed gel
plugged views of my pluck and offal.
Some accident had released flora

who live in us and will eat us
when we stop feeding them the earth.
I'd rehearsed the private office of the grave,
ceased excreting, made corpse gases

all while liana'd in tubes
and overseen by cockpit instruments
that beeped or struck up Beethoven's
Fifth at behests of fluid.

I also hear when I lay lipless
and far away I was anointed
first by a mild metaphoric church
then by the Church of no metaphors.

Now I said, signing a Dutch contract
in a hand I couldn't recognise,
let's go and eat Chinese soup
and drive to Lake Macquarie. Was I

not renewed as we are in Heaven?
In fact I could hardly endure
Earth gravity, and stayed weak and cranky
till the soup came, squid and vegetables,

pure Yang. And was sane thereafter.
It seemed I'd also travelled
in a Spring-in-Winter love-barque of cards,
of flowers and phone calls and letters,

concern I'd never dreamed was there
when black kelp boiled in my head.
I'd awoken amid my State funeral,
nevermore to eat my liver

or feed it to the Black Dog, depression
which the three Johns Hunter seem
to have killed with their scalpels:
it hasn't found its way home,

where I now dodder and mend
in thanks for devotion, for the ambulance
this time, for the hospital fork lift,
for pethidine, and this face of deity:

not the foreknowledge of death
but the project of seeing conscious life
rescued from death defines and will
atone for the human.

A Deployment of Fashion

In Australia, a lone woman
is being crucified by the Press
at any given moment.

With no unedited right
of reply, she is cast out
into Aboriginal space.

It's always for a defect in weeping:
she hasn't wept on cue
or she won't weep correctly.

There's a moment when the sharks are
still butting her, testing her protection,
when the Labor Party, or influence,

can still save her. Not the Church,
not other parties. Even at that stage
few men can rescue her.

Then she goes down, overwhelmed
in the feasting grins of pressmen,
and Press women who've moved

from being owned by men
to being owned by fashion,
these are more deeply merciless.

She is rogue property,
she must be taught her weeping.
It is done for the millions.

Sometimes the millions join in
with jokes: how to get a baby
in the Northern Territory? Just stick

your finger down a dingo's throat.
Most times, though, the millions
stay money, and the jokes

are snobbish media jokes:
Chemidenko. The Oxleymoron.
Spittle, like the flies on Black Mary.

After the feeding frenzy
sometimes a ruefully balanced last lick
precedes the next selection.

The Holy Show

I was a toddler, wet-combed
with my pants buttoned to my shirt
and there were pink and green lights, pretty
in the day, a Christmas-tree party
up the back of the village store.

I ran towards it, but big sad people
stepped out. They said over me *It's just, like,*
for local kiddies and *but let him join in*;
the kiddies looked frightened
and my parents, caught off guard

one beat behind me, grabbed me up
in the great shame of our poverty
that they talked about to upset themselves.
They were blushing and smiling, cursing me
in low voices *Little bugger bad boy!*

for thinking happy Christmas undivided,
whereas it's all owned, to buy in parcels
and have at home; for still not knowing
you don't make a holy show of your family;
outside it, there's only parry and front.

Once away, they angrily softened to
me squalling, because I was their kiddie
and had been right about the holy show
that models how the world should be
and could be, shared, glittering in near focus

right out to the Sex frontier.

Death from Exposure

That winter. We missed her stark face
at work. Days till she was found, under

his verandah. Even student torturers
used to go in awe. She had zero small talk.

It made no sense she had his key.
It made no sense all she could have

done. Depression exhausts the mind.
She phones, no response, she drives up

straight to his place in the mountains,
down a side road, frost all day.

You knock. What next? You can't manage
what next. Back at last, he finds her car.

She's crawled in, under, among the firewood.
Quite often the world is not round.

The Averted

The one whose eyes
do not meet yours
is alone at heart
and looks where the dead look
for an ally in his cause.

Panic Attack

The body had a nightmare.
Awake. No need of the movie.

No need of light, to keep hips
and shoulders rotating in bed
on the gimbals of wet eyes.

Pounding heart, chest pains –
should it be the right arm hurting?

The brain was a void
or a blasted-out chamber –
shreds of speech in there,
shatters of lust and prayer.

No one can face their heart
or turn their back on it.

Bowel stumbled to bowl,
emptied, and emptied again
till the gut was a train
crawling in its own tunnel,

slowly dragging the nightmare
down with it, below heart level.
You would not have died

the fear had been too great
but: to miss the ambulance moment –

Relax. In time, your hourglass
will be reversed again.

Refusing Saul's Armour

i.m. Lex Banning, poet, 1921–65

x times y marks the spot
where my maths hit the wall.
It was all x from there.
In my last school exam
I drew maths on the paper

and Higher Studies were critique
but my mind was a groover
and a fiver a week
postponed me as a lover,
masking my terror

of sex and employment.
Films and unset books engrossed me.
As scorn soured play, I slept
in buildings and long grass.
Faith and tobacco still

kept the Black Dog at bay,
and blind-tapping down Ashbury
the Pill taught him no kindness:
his bared-teeth smile came
as all turned to hope and blame

and our spastic model poet
agile in his narrow flat
showed us his sword collection.
Shame on bellies sucked in:
his stung blades knew their paladin.

Index of First Lines

Index of Titles